INSANELY INTRICATE
Shall We Dance?

COLORING BOOK

PHILL EVANS

DOVER PUBLICATIONS, INC.
MINEOLA, NEW YORK

No need to get out your dancing shoes to enjoy this amazing artwork! These dynamic dance designs feature diverse styles from ballet and ballroom to hip hop and hula, and everything in between! Each incredible image is perfect for the experienced colorist to bring to life with colored pencils or markers, and the unbacked pages are perforated to make displaying finished pages easy.

For an added challenge, look for the artist's name—Phill Evans—creatively hidden within each of the dazzling designs.

Bibliographical Note
Insanely Intricate Shall We Dance? Coloring Book is a new work, first published by Dover Publications, Inc., in 2016.

International Standard Book Number
ISBN-13: 978-0-486-80461-3
ISBN-10: 0-486-80461-5

Manufactured in the United States by RR Donnelley
80461501   2016
www.doverpublications.com

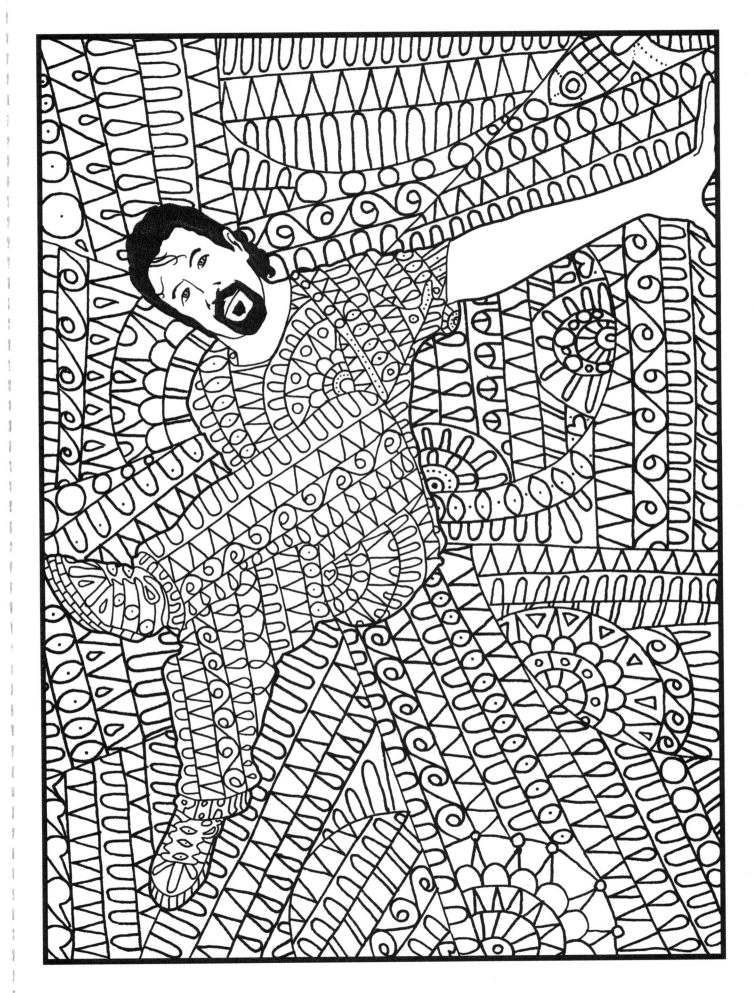

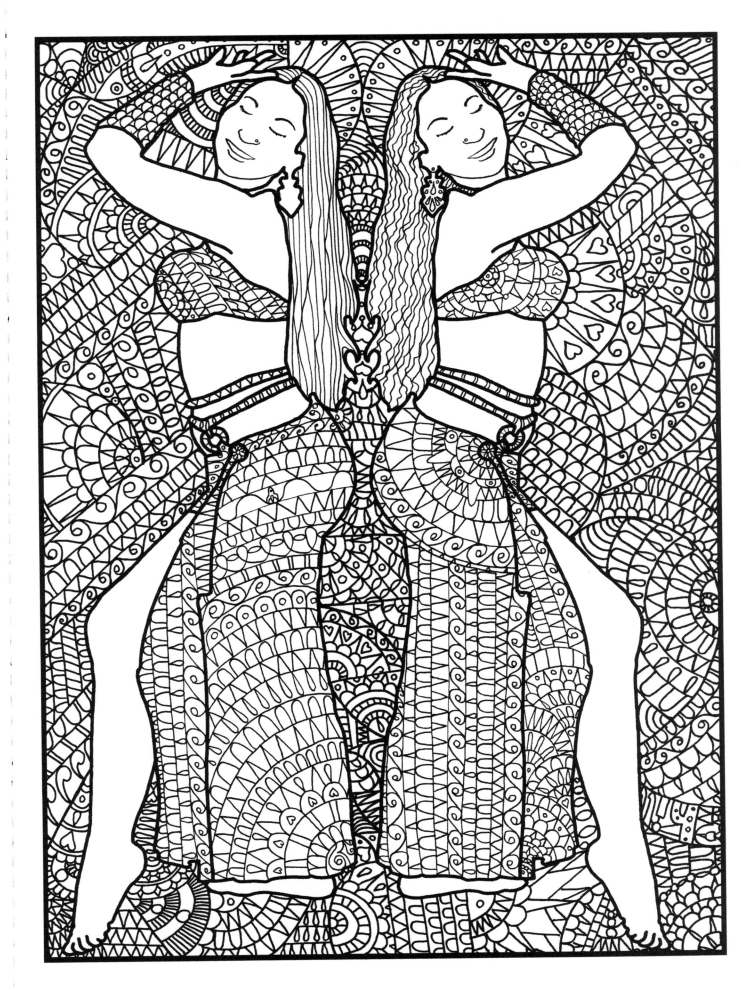

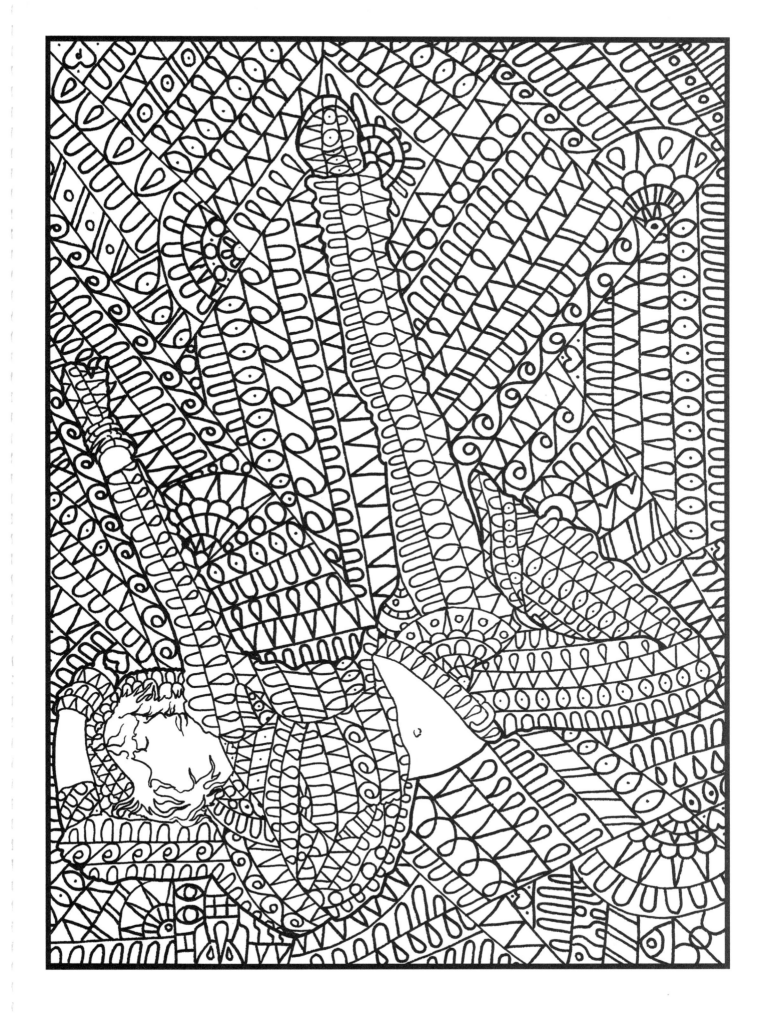

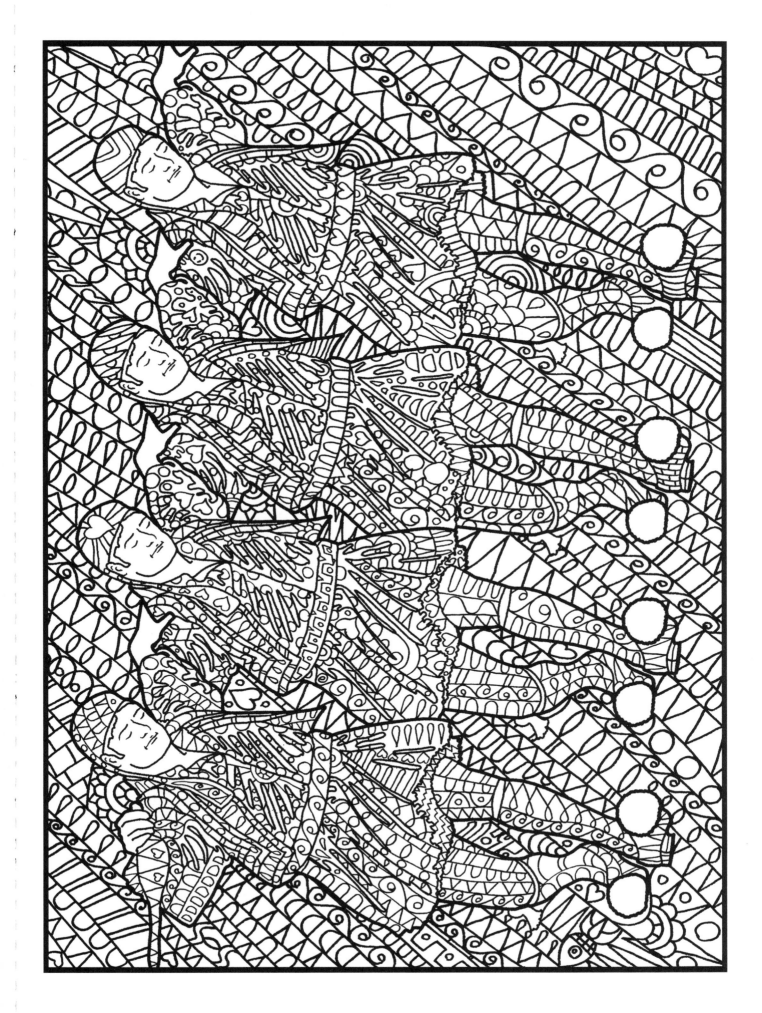

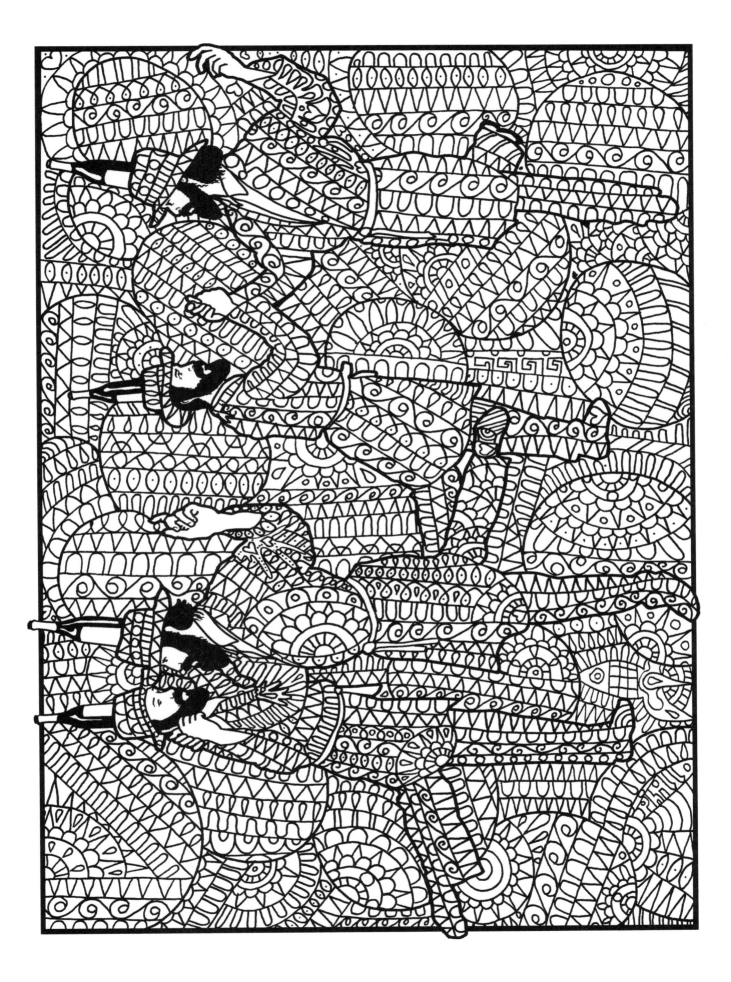

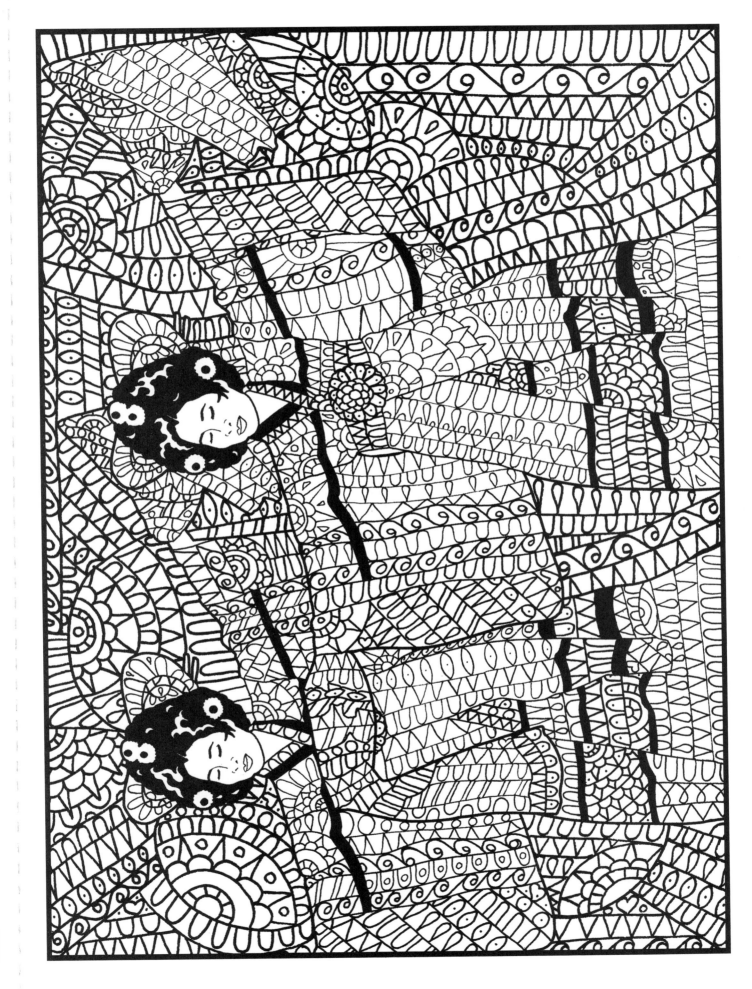

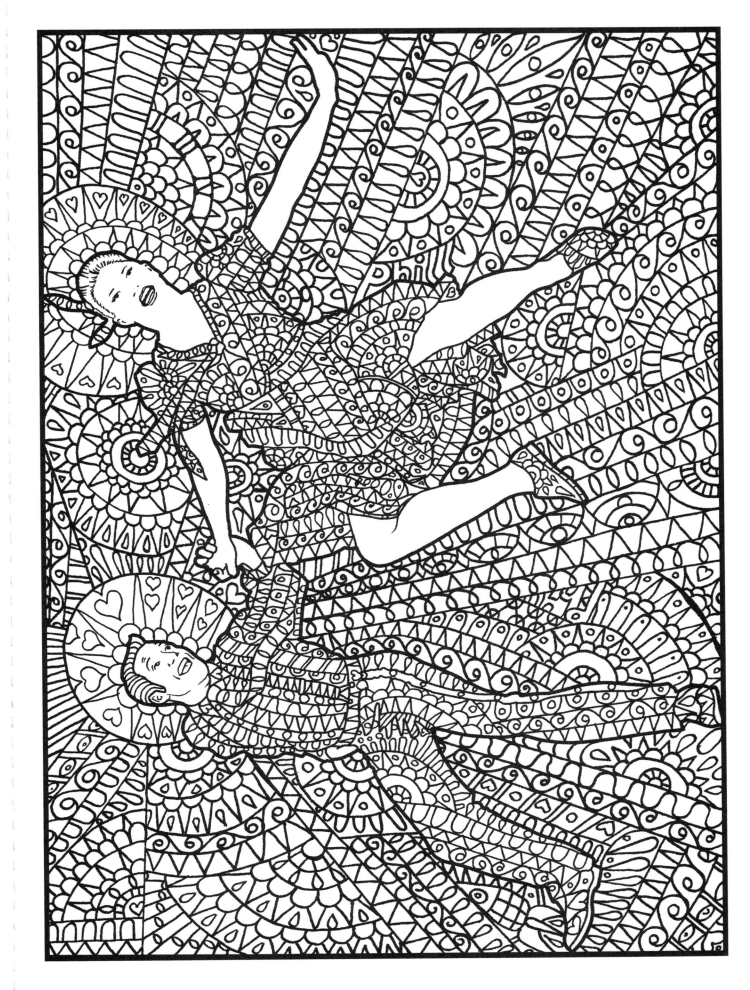